Love Psalms to God

For My Husband

When You Are Single and Waiting

Teresa A. Stith

Love Psalms to God for My Husband

Copyright © 2020 Teresa A. Stith

All rights reserved. This book is protected by the copyright laws of the United States of America. This book may not be copied or reprinted for commercial gain or profit. The use of short quotations or occasional page copying for personal or group study is permitted and encouraged. Permission will be granted upon request.

Unless otherwise identified, scripture quotations are from the King James Version of the Bible. Copyright © 1982 by Thomas Nelson, Inc. Used by permission. All rights reserved.

Please note that certain pronouns referring to the Father, Son, and Holy Spirit may be capitalized to acknowledge God and any such titles referring to Him. Please note just the opposite when referring to satan. We choose not to capitalize his name or acknowledge him in any way, even to the point of violating grammatical rules.

ISBN-13: 978-1-7332744-3-2

Publisher- A Faith That Works Publishing

Website: afaiththatworks.com

You made all the delicate,

inner parts of my body

and knit me together in my mother's womb

Thank you for making me

so wonderfully complex!

Your workmanship is marvelous-

how well do I know it!

Psalms 139:13-14

-New Living Translation

I have waited for you my love

for much of my adult life.

I have entertained many men in my lifetime

trying to become their wife.

Each one hurt me differently

and my scars are the proof

That patience had her perfect work

Because I now have you.

I'll hold you in my memory

Until God sees fit to release

This gift of love that I call HUSBAND

An Astounding Masterpiece!

DEDICATION

This book is dedicated to all of you Queens who, if you are anything like me, have desired a husband for quite some time now. Our reasons for not having one yet may differ, but I hope that I can maybe shed some light on some things that we should be doing while we are waiting. It is also my desire that this book will help you come to terms with some things in your life that you may need to tell good-bye. To embrace this new life with your husband, you will definitely need to walk away from old flings, past hurts, a jealous heart, revengeful spirits, and unforgiveness. It's impossible to move forward in faith, in peace or in love with these negative attachments. If it's your desire to hold on to them, then this book is not for you. God cannot pour new wine into old bottles! So you have to decide now if you are ready for who He is about to send into your life. Stop looking for flaws in a man, humph you have some. Some of us may have already missed our husbands looking for the perfect man, he's not out here! If a man is willing to overlook your flaws to love you, then who are you to point out and not accept his because they conflict with you? If some of us do not learn to get over ourselves, we will be by ourselves for a very long time. Remember, YOU are why you are single. It is nobody else's fault. I used to say that "I am single by choice". That was the biggest lie! The truth was that this *lie* was my safety net and it really held me together mentally as I considered what in the world was wrong, the reason why I could not seem to find love and keep it. At least it made me feel that I was still somehow in control of my life and who I wanted to have in it. Nobody was knocking my door down, ringing my phone, or asking me out on dates so I was very comfortable walking around looking evil all of the time, and who wanted to deal with that? Nobody wanted these problems, and of course after being sick and tired of smelling my own self for a while literally, I decided that it was time to wash my attitude and rid myself of that and all of the other filth that was making men go the other way when they saw me, and change some things about myself. I did not realize how angry I was! I was mad about everything! I was mad that I was single, I was mad about my own personal battles and struggles in life, and I was mad that it seemed as though I never had the resources available to help me. I was mad that I did not get to cry a lot during this season because I had to be strong and endure. So let me take a moment now to finally…scream!!!!!

  Now, it is not that men have never tried to approach me, but my defense mechanisms were so strong because of the last man that hurt me, that the one who was trying to steal my heart got worn out from trying and eventually chose to go elsewhere. Ladies look, we must shake loose from our past. We need to go on and accept the fact that love was not meant to happen for us at that particular time and our singleness is now a direct result of that. The Bible tells us that "to every thing there is a season, and a time to every purpose under heaven" (Ecclesiastes 3:1). We bring these unfortunate situations into our lives when we fail to wait on our proper seasons. Because we want love now, we make a mess of our lives with our wrong choices in men (or women) and suffer brokenness as a result. Stop trying to make the pieces that other people hold fit into the puzzle of your life. It won't work! It's funny how we know that certain people won't work in our lives and we still pursue them like there's some missing part of us that appear to be attracted to the foolishness in them. It's not the end of the world people, let that mess go. Some people have gone as far as they need to go in your life, bid them farewell, and proceed to LIVE! Those unfortunate events (if you will) should teach us or should have taught us, to be careful how we hear and embrace wisdom, knowledge, and understanding. Let's release back into the atmosphere the sweetness of a love that only we know that we possess. For a man to know, he has to be invited into your space. You have to grant him access to you up close and personal so that he can learn to value your worth. You may be making it a little hard for him to see this from a distance.

  This book is about Love Psalms to God for your husband, and I will be singing my butt off when God finally unwraps this gift of love and present me with His excellent choice of a man for me. Are *we* ready?

When I wasn't looking, you came into my life

When I wasn't seeking,

You were praying for a wife

I thought my life was over

But little did I know

That you were somewhere waiting

For the Lord to tell you "GO"

Throughout my season of waiting

I have prayed for you

Knowing full well what I am in for

Because you are praying too

God has shown us favor

By allowing us to meet

Now we're singing Psalms together

Because now we're both COMPLETE!

The Wait Is Over! God is about to present you with a package that only you know how to handle. HANDLE with care and rejoice!

♥♥♥♥♥♥

TABLE OF CONTENTS

1. Preparing For My Husband……….…...1
2. Too Old For What?......................................13
3. Love Psalms…………………………....…..25
4. Don't Chase, Get Chosen……………..….. 31
5. Praying For Your Husband…………....…41
6. Obeying God Intentionally……….….……49
7. Living God's Way…Purposefully……..…55
8. Financially Free?……………………….…...63
9. What the Bible Says About Love………………………………………......69
10. Your Single Self……………………......…75
About the Author………………………………79
More Information………………………………80
New and Upcoming Titles.……………………81

HUSBAND

No more shopping alone.
No more cooking just enough for me.
No more seeing others holding hands
and wishing that it was us.
No more going to the movies alone.
No more sleeping by myself and
rolling over to the wall.
No more traveling alone.
No more sharing my hopes and dreams
with the mirror.
Come and take your place my King.
You have given me hope and I'm here for it!

Preparing For My Husband
1

OMG! Is my hair straight? Is my makeup right? Did I make my nail appointment? Take out the garbage? Is my room straight? I don't have time to....

This has been a season of expectation for me. I have finally come to a place in my life where I am preparing myself to meet my husband. The years have flown by and there were times that I actually thought that I may not get married. I felt that I had gotten too old, and that surely nobody wanted someone who was set in their ways, controlling, and not about to take any mess off of a man! I have gone back and forth with the Lord many times about him, but when my heart began to "yearn" for him, I knew that God was positioning me to receive this long awaited PRIZE. He is preparing me for my husband.

Let's go back a little bit. I got married the first time when I was only 21 years of age. I saw an opportunity to "get out of the house" basically, and I jumped at it despite my Leaders' instructions (disobedient). They kept telling me to wait. Wait for what? I was tired of waiting. I was tired of living at home and saw an opportunity to leave my mother's house and start a life of my own, so I took it. I tell you what, after all of the dust settled from that whirlwind of a marriage, with the little bit of sanity I had left, I decided to wait on the Lord. Let me just mention that I did love my husband, but my definition of love was what I perceived love to be at that time. It was more about morals and doing the right thing in a marriage than it was about love and honoring my marriage because of how God viewed it.

Love Psalms to God

Marriage was honorable to the Lord, and being so young, I did not know anything about love, but you couldn't tell me that at the time. For all I knew, lust was love. At 21 it *seemed* to be working…until it wasn't. It did not take me long to figure that out! Had I just paid attention and listened, I would not have gone through all of the extremes that came with being broken because I wanted love right then.

Now, waiting for me was not easy. First of all, I loved fornicating! Now do you all want me to be real or what? If you cannot be real about where you are, you'll have problems getting to where you are trying to go! I had not allowed myself the chance to be completely delivered from the lust of the flesh, sexual sins, and things of that nature, so waiting was stressful. My will, my desire, and my CHOICE to have sex kept pulling me down in sin. I would win some battles, sustain myself, and fall a little harder the next time. This cycle went on for years until I was finally ready to stop devaluing myself because I wanted to feel good for a few minutes. I had to make that decision. There was never any real commitment to living right at that time (problem #1) because I was still learning who I was. There were still things that I was experiencing and learning about myself and about life. It was tough for me. I could not seem to get this part of my life right, and the worthlessness that I felt within from so many failed relationships and failed attempts at love began to take its toll on me, and I spiraled into a state of depression. I wondered why I could not find someone that wanted to make me theirs, but the truth was, I wasn't ready. The more I focused on what was wrong with me, the more **I saw** *that was wrong* with me. I had been so badly broken, scarred, and hurt that those things had become sort of a place of safety for me. I hid behind them because I wasn't ready to face my truth. My truth was, that I did not want to commit to anything, but I wanted to control everything. Being promiscuous led me down some dark paths and impacted my relationship with people who I would go to war for now, BUT GOD!

    I began to repent of my sins before God and start the road to recovery by taking a good look at myself. I didn't want to face the deeper issues that I was trying so desperately to hide from, but God could not deliver me if I didn't want to see. So I slowly gave myself away to Him and began to release the hurt, pain, and guilt of sin to Him so that He could make me healthy, healed, and WHOLE! Won't He do it?

Teresa A. Stith

**WAIT A MINUTE
WHILE I DELIVER MYSELF
IN THESE PAGES!!!**

Are You Ready Mentally?

God is not going to send you a husband until He knows that you are ready. Being ready has nothing to do with your life being perfect. He wants to know if your heart is ready. Have you prepared your mind to accept this *change?* I know that you have been controlling much of your life, but are you ready to relinquish that control to the "Head" of your household, because it is no longer you?

Love Psalms to God

"Ain't no man telling me what to do"
"I'm not picking up behind no man"
"I'm not cooking every night"
"Hmmm, I sure hope he knows how to do something!"
"I hope he's good in bed"
"Lord you know what I need"

This was me at one point, griping and complaining about the kind of man that I wanted God to give me. I had no earthly idea that I was worried about the wrong things. I was still trying to satisfy my flesh to some extent by making these worldly requests and not considering what my husband may be needing from me (mistake #2). Besides that, what was he asking God for in a wife? Look, the marriage won't be about you alone, it will be about you both. You both will make a commitment to serve one another because marriage is both a ministry and a service so SERVE one another with gladness!

For as long as I can remember, I have had to cut my own grass, cook, clean, take care of my kids, make major decisions, learn how to trust, etc. all without the help or guidance from a man. It's easy to become rather independent in this respect. I think that for me, my mentality towards the whole marriage thing will be the biggest challenge. Trusting someone else to do these things or even help, will all be new for myself and some of you but, don't you think you deserve to hand the reins over now? You are now a help meet for your husband, so help him…but he is ultimately responsible for making sure that the home is well taken care of, let him do that.

Love Psalms to God

Are You Ready To Commit?

If you know that you are not ready to commit to a man or a marriage, do not get married. If you know that you still like sneaking around, do not get married. If you still have feelings for a past lover, do not get married. If you have roaming eyes, do not get married! Don't set yourself or the man you want to marry up by entering a marriage knowing full well that you still plan to live like you were prior to marriage. Be considerate of one another's feelings. This is for you single men too! Remember, marriage is a ministry and God loves and honors marriage. Be sincere about why you want to be married and then commit your marriage unto the Lord. If God is at the forefront of your marriage, you never have to worry about the enemy slipping in unaware. God will reveal when you two need to talk, when you need to listen, when you need to come together, and when you need to pray, etc. The key here is not forgetting that you were married in the eyesight of God. If you live in your marriage and remember that God is there too, things will be perfect because HE is perfect and He loves LOVE! Trust in God's timing. It is always better to wait awhile and have things fall into place, than to rush and have things fall apart later.

> Your love is like a magnet,
> I'm drawn to it constantly
> I'm feeling things that only you
> can make me feel.
> YOU ARE my delight,
> my manna from on high.
> God did His thing and I'm grateful that
> He chose you for me.

Lord help me to step whole-heartedly into this divine place of rest. Of sweet love, of life and happiness…of YOU.

Love Psalms to God

"Two are better than one,
because they have a good return
for their labor:
If either of them falls down, one
can help the other up.
But pity anyone who falls and
has no one to help them up.
Also, if two lie down together,
they will keep warm.
But how can one keep warm alone?"
Ecclesiastes 4:9

Thank you Lord for my "Husband"

Teresa A. Stith

NOW LET'S DIG A LITTLE DEEPER WE'RE JUST GETTING STARTED!

Too Old For What?

 I had given up on ever getting married again, feeling like I was too old to even think about a husband at this age. I honestly think that I had convinced myself that I was okay alone, until the desire for a husband began to creep into my heart. I really hadn't given a lot of thought to it until recently when I began to find myself yearning for his companionship. I prayed genuinely this time to ask God to erase what I had said previously about it not mattering whether I had him or not. I wanted my husband! I thought about all of the trips that we would take together, how we would laugh at one another's crazy jokes, and even how we would study and pray together. I could not wait to share my life with the man that God had chosen for me. To show God how serious I was, I began to pray earnestly for my husband. I found myself praying that God leads him to me. That we fall in love instantly and that the Holy Ghost would be so involved in the process that we both would know right away that we belonged to each other. God has the final say so in determining what transpires in our lives. We say things out of our mouths all of the time, but isn't it good to know that God knows what is in our hearts? Age is only a number to Him. We are all familiar with the story of Abraham and Sarah and how God told Abraham that Sarah would be "a mother of nations" (Genesis 17:16) and that she would conceive and bear a son in her old age, but Sarah did not believe. Sarah did however, give birth to Isaac, just as God had promised and she was 90 years of age. This gave me hope that although it has not happened yet, God is still in control of our

Love Psalms to God

destinies. Look, don't be angry with God because it has not happened for you yet. Considering the emotional state that some of us were/are in, we wouldn't have been any good for a husband or ourselves, going into a marriage already broken. We should be glad that God made us wait.

> Lord, sanctify my eyes that
> they see only my husband.
> Hide my flaws behind Your grace.
> Bless me with the mind to know
> that I am one with my husband
> and that I am not competing against him.
> I am not jealous of him…
> He is mine
> And I am his.

You would be surprised at how many marriages bleed because spouses are in competition with one another. Who makes more money or who has the largest bank account is irrelevant when all of the household finances should be serving the same purpose. While we are waiting on our husbands, we should have grown in these areas. In my old age, I can still be a little bit demanding. I've been weaning myself from things that I like to control and I've been practicing saying "ok babe" because I have to be considerate of my husband's opinions. There will be things that he will do that I am sure will pluck my nerves at times, but I am practicing showing love anyway, and not taking everything so personal. Ladies, don't let your singleness damage you in a way that makes you an unlikely candidate for marriage. GROW. With age comes wisdom. Some things that you were doing as a child, you should be doing differently as an adult, so there are less arguments about who is right or wrong. There should be more periods where we learn to say

Love Psalms to God

"I love you" and "I apologize" rather than laying down angry, or looking for an opportunity to retaliate. That's not something that you do when you are married. That's something that you do when you cohabitate or lust after someone and have not been made perfect in love. But LOVE covers a multitude of sins! If my husband loves God, I know that he will love me. He may not be perfect, but I know that he was perfectly crafted for me. I will know my worth and my value to him and he will appreciate my virtuality…

    Praise God for a wonderful Gem!

Teresa A. Stith

"I acknowledge my transgressions;

and my sin is ever before me."

Sin that is unconfessed

shuts out the energies of grace.

Confession makes the soul receptive of

the bountiful waters of life.

We open the door to God as soon as

we name our sin.

Guilt that is penitently confessed

is already in the "consuming fire"

of God's love.

-John Henry Jowett

Love Psalms to God

So I battled the thoughts of my age being a crucial factor in becoming a wife again to the point of almost giving up on love. I'd actually convinced myself that it was too late. I stopped hoping that it would happen. I got used to sleeping by myself, preparing meals for myself, and getting in my car and going whenever I got ready with no questions asked. Men showed interest in me and I of course thought that it was cute, but never took any of them seriously. I thought to myself "humph, I still got it" (laugh out loud) but literally brushed it off like "who would be interested in my old self?" (laugh out loud).

I had become too comfortable in not expecting or looking to meet anyone. I literally stopped dressing up when I went outside of the house. I wasn't trying to impress anyone, and I certainly was not trying to draw any unwanted attention to myself. But no matter how I looked, the men always seemed to notice. I thought it was the devil lol because the goal was to NOT be noticed. I acted like I didn't see them looking, but I chuckled inside. Telling them in my heart to keep right on looking because that was about as much of me as they were going to get. It got so bad that one day, as I got in my car to go to the store, the Lord Himself made me go back into the house and change my clothes (laugh out loud). I needed to make a quick run to the store and so I jumped up like I have many days before, with my pajamas on, and slippers, grabbed my pocketbook and keys, and out the door I went. "I was coming right back," I thought. As soon as I put the key in the ignition, I heard the Holy Spirit say "go in the house and put on some clothes." I sit there for a minute because I did not want to go and change my clothes, I was coming right back. I had become lazy. I was set in my ways. I had become accustomed to going out looking any kind of way because I had allowed the devil to kill my expectation of ever being married again or just simply meeting someone nice. I did not care about being seen by a man or anyone else, but at that moment the Lord reassured me that just because I did not care about being seen when I went out, did not mean that I wouldn't be. Besides, I was still wearing HIS name, and if I didn't dress up for anyone else, I ought to always look my best for Him! Period. After that, I began to pay a little bit more attention to how I dressed when I stepped out, but it wasn't long before I began to sink into that "I'm not trying to impress anybody mentality" again. God help me!

God knows the plans that He has for us, they're not evil but good, to give us hope and a future (Jeremiah 29:11). We cannot hurry God, neither can we dictate to Him or make Him change the order of our lives to suit what we think we need. He knows what is best for us, and He knows who will be best at bringing out the best in us. The old mothers in the church used to say "If we just let God be God, everything will work out okay." Don't ask God "why?" instead, ask Him "what" is it that He wants you to learn and to "do" in the midst of what is happening. What has God said to you in your singleness? Have you been listening? Or have you been trying to control your own destiny? The thing about God is that He sees you, and He sees your husband. He knows where you are, and He knows where your husband is. While He works on bringing you two together, you should be making preparation for the day that you two meet. What a wonderful analogy! If this does not give you hope in knowing that your husband is out there, I don't know what will. Find your motivation girl and make preparation for your husband. Take out all of that trash from yesteryear and open your heart fully to LOVE. Don't entertain another thought about who did you wrong, or why they did it, that phase of your life is over! Embrace this season of newness and girl…get yourself together!

Teresa A. Stith

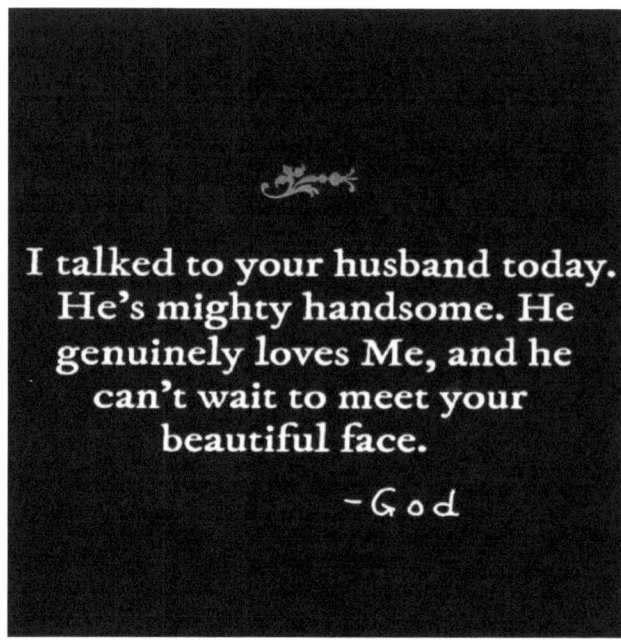

The Wait Is Over!

God is about to present you

with a package that only you know

how to handle.

HANDLE with care and rejoice!

Love Psalms

And be not drunken with wine,

wherein is riot,

but be filled with the Spirit;

speaking one to another in psalms and hymns

and spiritual songs,

singing and making melody with your heart

to the Lord; giving thanks always for

all things…

-Ephesians 5:18-20

I've often heard the statement that a drunk man will tell all of his business. I've also heard that a drunk man will tell the truth about his business and yours too, if he knows it. I know for a fact that a drunk man can also sing his butt off. He may not be making any sense to you or me, but he be singing like there's no tomorrow and not having a care in the world how he sounds, or that he may be a little off key. What he knows in that moment is that his heart is satisfied, free, happy, and in a place of contentment, and he does not want to be bothered. He doesn't owe anybody any explanation about why he is here. He just wants to enjoy the moment. Have you ever tried to stop a drunk man from singing? You'd almost have to fight him! So then what was it about the song that meant so much to him? Was he simply recalling a time in his life that was good? Or was it even about the song at all?

"Forever in my heart is where you will be
Nobody else will enter because
you have the only key"
-Adrian Jackson

Love Psalms to God

While I never fully understood a drunk man's reason for singing when he drank, I've learned to listen to my own heart while waiting for my husband. I've learned how to make a melody in my heart that was so passionate for him, that God would listen intently to my heart's plea and answer me accordingly. My desire for my husband became breakfast, lunch, and dinner. I began to look for him in the streets and in the stores. I wasn't sure in which direction he would come, so I made myself ready on all sides. I took a little extra time to get dressed in the morning and comb my hair. I made sure that I looked good and smelled good. I looked for him literally and desired him as if he would be here any minute. Isn't this what the Bible tells us to do? The Bible says that when we pray, we must believe that we have already received, and then we shall have what we say (Mark 11:24). Amen.

Even though God knows what things we stand in need of before we pray, He still urges us to be specific in prayer. In Matthew 20: 29-34, we come on the scene with 2 blind men who hears that Jesus is passing by. They began to cry out saying "Lord, have mercy on us." Jesus asks them, "what do you want me to do for you?" And they replied "Lord, open our eyes." It was at this point that Jesus heals their sight. Your love psalm to God should be so unique and pure that even the angels in Heaven gasp at the deepness of it. For it is here, that you pour out your most sincere and earnest request and where God hears your heart's cry for love. He knows this love language all too well because He is love. God put love in every vessel and vein that He placed within us. He was so careful with His handling of us, that He knows how many hairs He put on our heads. I don't want to just talk this love language, I want it to show in my walk and how I behave while waiting for my husband. When he sees me, he will recognize the language. He will be able to "read" me from afar and we will dance to the beat of our own drums and sanctify our love for one another. Through the beat of our hearts intertwined, our love will be threaded together with an unfeigned value and respect for how this ministry of joy has found and arrested our union. This will be a Holy matrimony between us as friends, but also as lovers.

Prayer: Lord, sanctify my prayer and search my insides. I desire my husband like I do a cold cup of water on a hot summer day. Only the Light of Your love can quench this thirst. Oh sing my heart, sing! Amen.

Teresa A. Stith

I'll sing psalms to the Lord Most High and
pray that He won't pass me by
The smallest detail I'll share with Him
For there's no secret hidden from Him
I'll make melody in my heart to the Lord
And let my husband finish the chord
It is him who completes me, But it is God
Who completes us
And through Him, WE ARE ONE
He is me and I am he
and together…We are US….

A LOVE PSALM

Don't Chase, Get Chosen

"The single biggest problem in communication is the illusion that it has taken place."
-George Bernard Shaw

    Men have a tendency sometimes to think that women are saying something that they may not be saying which causes a misunderstanding in communication. One of the things that I have found to be challenging in this season of life is to ensure that what I am communicating to men is exactly what I mean. People in general tend to respond to non-verbal communications just as quickly as they do to verbal communication, so we have to make sure that we are speaking a language that not only men, but everyone else clearly understands. Our facial expressions, eye contact or lack thereof, and body movements may be sending a message that may come back to bite us later on, such as what happened to me.

Unbeknownst to me at the time, (in my younger years) because I was unaware of the effectiveness of nonverbals, men began to tell me that I had bedroom eyes. I mean, I was hearing this on a regular basis from one man after another. Oh, I was furious and took my stance against what I perceived to be a label on me. I was ready to fight to defend my honor because I knew who I was. I thought that men were low key calling me out of my name and referring to me as being something that I clearly did not associate myself with until one guy explained to me what the expression meant. No matter how he sliced and diced it, I made it clear that men should not refer to me in that manner. This caused me to be conscious of how I moved when I was around men. It's easy to send wrong or inappropriate messages to men that were not our intention to send, and depending on where he is in his life, that may be perceived as inviting or saying something that we may not be saying. Just be careful how you entertain other people. You may be asking well, "why were you so offended?" I was offended because at one point in my life, I probably did have bedroom eyes, considering the fact that I was very promiscuous in my younger years. After I had given my life to Christ and changed my ways, I still had to work to maintain my integrity. And while that is no longer my lifestyle, I do not care to be associated with or identified with it any longer. We have to know when to put the axe to the root and cut stuff off. We must realize that we have an adversary out here…the devil…and he is always seeking ways to make us look like we have no hope, or no choice…so we sin against God, but we ALL know that he is a liar!

Knowing that at one point in my life men were considered my weakness, why would the devil then send men to tell me that I had bedroom eyes? Because he would very much like for me to fall back down into that unhealthy lifestyle so that he can run to God and accuse me of sin. The Bible calls him "an accuser of the brethren." (Revelation 12:10). The devil will always accuse us of something. Only don't let what he is telling God about you be true, which brings me to the title of this chapter…Don't Chase, Get Chosen!

Love Psalms to God

I used to love the attention that I received from men. It used to make me feel like I was worth something and it made me feel good about myself. I didn't know anything about being unequally yoked or desiring someone who was compatible with me, I just wanted the attention. Only desiring attention from a man, led me to some messed up places in life and I got involved with some very dangerous people. Thank God for keeping me in my ignorance. Having grown to know God personally, I understand that I can have what I ask Him for. So I've learned to ask for only what I know will please the Father. I will not ask for a man who does not love the Lord or who is not striving to be like the Lord. I will not ask God for a man who abuses women or fails to fellowship with others who are striving to be like Christ. I need a man who has a heart after God because if he loves the Lord, I know that he will be a perfect match for me so, don't chase, get chosen. Know your worth! Know that God desires to give you what you are asking for when it lines up with His will for your life. Never feel like you have to chase a guy down. If it is meant to be, it will happen for you. Don't seem too desperate in your singleness!

I used to feel like all of the "good guys" were taken, but then I had to consider that there must be "one more" because I'm still waiting on mine! It is this hope that keeps me not only expecting, but using my single time to clean up residue from my past that would have no place in a new life with my husband. What you think you need, you probably already have. God is not going to give you something that will bring more heartache than joy. It is often our own choices that causes conflict with God's plans for our lives and because we do not want to wait on Him, we run into the devastation of hasty decisions in our choice for love. How foolish and messed up I was to even fathom in my mind at one point in my life that God would give me someone else's husband. Was I that badly broken that I could not think intelligently enough to desire my own? Looking back at these things and all of the friendships and relationships that were tainted because of my irresponsibility, I was quite ashamed. Now I know that part of my singleness is due to the decisions that I made in the past and that although God forgave me, I still had to learn from them. Would you agree? I can honestly say that I believe that God has smiled on my faithfulness to allow Him to repair and mend those difficult areas of my life and trust that He has a husband out here looking for me. As I continue to be about my Father's business, He will find me. And just to cover myself, if he doesn't find me in this lifetime, IT IS WELL with my soul! So the only One that I really need to chase is YOU O' God! I'm in hot pursuit of Your love, Your grace I would not recognize my need for a husband Unless You awaken Your Spirit in me.

Search me, O' God, and **know my heart:**
try me,
and know my thoughts:
And see if there be any wicked way in me,
and lead me in the way everlasting
(Psalm 139:23-24).

You will never have to chase a man or woman who says that they love you. They will always want to be where you are. Love is mutual, so someone that you say that you love should never have to chase you. Genuine love draws you to one another. It boasts of its relationship with you and is infatuated with you in a righteous way. This kind of love is preserved.

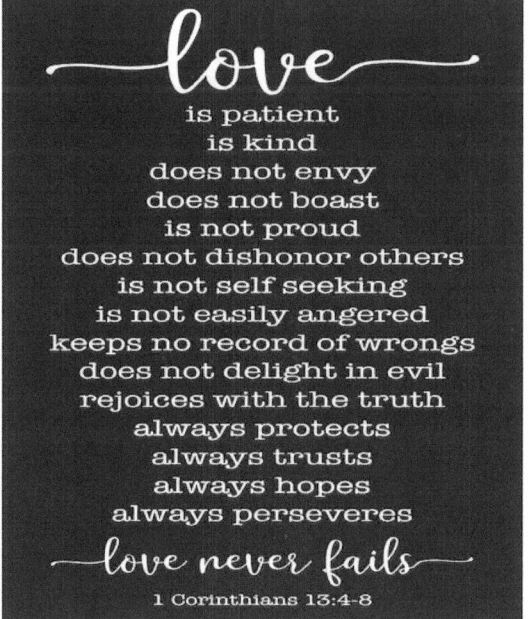

Teresa A. Stith

GOD DESIGNED LOVE WITH YOU IN MIND. HE'S IN LOVE WITH YOU.

Praying For Your Husband
5

Begin now to pray for your husbands. Not so much for what you would like to see in him, but for what you both can contribute to one another. Pray that God allows you to be able to communicate effectively and resolve small matters that could become greater issues later. Pray that God comes in and be a focal point for your relationship or marriage. When you learn to include God in your personal business, all other business matters flourish. Invite God into your home, into your bedroom, your prayer closet, into your kitchen, and into any area of your life that the enemy may see as an invitation to wreak havoc and destroy what God is creating. Stop praying to marry the man you love, but rather pray to God that you love the man you are marrying! LOVE HIM…not

LUST after him! Don't mistake "good sex" for love. When men make us feel good in the bedroom, we (women) tend to call that "love". Let's make sure that we are calling it what it is "good sex" and a feel good moment, not "love". We cannot live a life of fornication and expect God to give us a husband. If we are not careful, we might marry immaturely and then cheat on our husbands because our marriage was not based on love, but "good sex" or "lust". All of these things must be taken into consideration before we go to God for a husband. First, we need to be clear on if we really do want a husband, or if we just want to be sexual or intimate with someone without the consequences of sin or fornication? And please don't ask God for a husband just so you can lay up and have sex!

    Being a single woman myself, I have had to make sure that my request for a husband to God was really what I wanted and not just a plea to God for companionship because at one time I felt that I was lonely. Some of us are single for this very reason. We would love to blame God for not having sent our husbands yet, but truth be told, if God were to give us our husbands prematurely, we would run him away ourselves because we did not allow the Holy Spirit to heal us completely before marriage. Remember, God knows us better than we know our own selves and He is preventing us from further hurt and pain by allowing us to confess our faults, and then giving us the time and space to be healed. We've complained about it taking so long to meet someone. We've complained about nobody looking at us. We've actually gotten upset with God because of all of the fake love that we have seen that *looks* real…like other couples are having the time of their lives. Not saying that *some* of them aren't, but the enemy knows how to get you to accuse God of some kind of wrongdoing by showing you false images of things that appear to be real.

I used to joke with some of my friends and coworkers whenever the topic came up about meeting a man. I used to say "well, there must be a hidden sign on my chest saying "keep it moving buddy" because men do not even stop to glance in my direction! I had to laugh at the thought that it could actually be true. So, I asked the Lord, "Lord, is there something on me (that I can't see) that You have placed on me, that when men see it, they don't stop or approach me to inquire if I'm single or not?" I haven't gotten an answer yet, laugh out loud…but I do KNOW that there's a special covering over and around me, and that God has His hands on my life, in my life and all over my husband, whomever he may be. I can honestly say that!

    Yearning for my husband led me to pray more earnestly for him. I often wonder what he is doing and what he is saying to God about me. I've learned to ask the Holy Ghost to teach me what I should be praying for my husband. In what areas does he need help? What is he trusting and believing God to do. I often wonder if he is funny or can sing his butt off! Will his voice be deep and powerful or smooth and soothing? Is he a worshipper or does he operate fully in the gifts of the Spirit? I am so super-ready and excited to see. I am ready to meet this man, but until God deems necessary, I will continue to pray, wait, and seek God's face for him. I can see the smile on his face as he holds my hands and tells me how long he has waited to meet his bride. I had a dream not long ago that I was in the room with so many preachers and ministers and mighty men of God. My own Pastor and First Lady was in the dream and others that I knew. It appeared that they were all gathered in this place as it was some kind of conference for those in ministry. Soon, it appeared that I was with a man but I could not see his face. I knew that he was a minister and I knew that he was my husband, but I just could not see his face. Oh how I have longed to see him! I have had dream after dream about seeing myself in ministry, speaking a Word to others, and prophesying and healing those who need healing. What does all of this mean? At least it helps me to understand what kind of man I should be seeking God for. I want a man who worships the Lord and recognizes God in every aspect of his life. I want a man who is not afraid to fall down on his knees and bombard Heaven with persistent prayer. But some things come through fasting and praying.

Love Psalms to God

Prayer: Lord, You know my desire for my husband, for the man that You have created me to yearn. A worshipper, a man who praises, a man after Your own heart. Lord teach me what I should be praying for as I wait to come into the fullness of all that You have planned for me. Strengthen my husband that he may be able to deal with my moodiness and crazy ways and prepare me to be strength for him in his time of need. Kill these emotions, that they will not hinder nor prevent us from yielding ourselves fully to Your purposes and plans. Furthermore Lord, invade our space and equip us and motivate us for Kingdom Advancement. Together Lord, we seek to be pleasing in Your sight. We want to take Your messages of love, joy, peace, hope and inspiration to a lost and dying world that they too will enjoy a right and righteous relationship with You. Perfect us Lord and make us suitable for the Kingdom. Give us a heart, a mind, and a love so great, that others will be drawn to it. We are so grateful for Your faithfulness to us always, so we strive daily to always please You. Prepare us for Heaven. Bind us together as ONE in You as we seek thy face continually. Amen.

Obeying God Intentionally

Something to remember as you make preparation for your husband, is to be intentional in obeying God. Continue to fast, continue to pray, and continue to seek the Lord for wisdom and instruction. Oftentimes, when we get what we have desired from the Lord, we tend to renege on our commitments or promises to Him. God did not change in our process of *growing* through, and we should not change when our prayers are manifested. Having a husband or responsibilities as a wife does not exclude us from obeying God and spending time in His word. This is our HELP. We should seek earnestly to obey Him even more. These are critical times because we need the power of the Holy Ghost to teach us how to maintain what God has given us. We have sought our husbands diligently through prayer and fasting, so we must honor God and show our appreciation to Him by continuing to be persistent in a life lived through obedience to the Father. God does not get moved to second place because you have a husband. Keep your priorities straight. God is the Author of this marriage, so let Him write the story as you sit back and read it. My Pastor used to say that "God don't tie no knots because knots come a-loose." He JOINS two people together, and what He joins together cannot be broken! As you stay committed to trusting God and obeying Him, the blessings of the Lord will overtake you. God loves to reward those who obeys Him. The blessings of the Lord goes far beyond finances. When God blesses you, He does it supernaturally in ways that you cannot fathom or reason in your own mind. God blesses you with those *jaw-dropping blessings*…those that leave you astonished for weeks! Abraham knows all too well about these kinds of blessings! See, he was well over the age of child-bearing and so was Sarah his wife, and they both laughed in their hearts at the idea of having a child at such an old age. But the Bible says that "Abraham believed in the Lord; and the Lord counted it to him for righteousness (Genesis 15:6). Abraham did not use his age as an excuse to not believe God, but rather held fast to the promise that God made. Going into a marriage or just making mental preparations for a marriage can be a very scary and draining process. You have been single for so long and you want to know that you have mastered this journey and are ready to step fully into this next phase of life. You have been equipped throughout the pages of this book and know how to conduct yourself as a wife and stay married in the process. You are stepping onto new territory and you just simply have to trust God now. Listen, while marriage may not be unknown territory for every one reading this book, how *we relate* to God in our marriage may be. There may be things that you learned from the first marriage or relationship that you could use here, but none of it works if it is not yielded to the Holy Spirit in faith. Remember, God (through the Holy Ghost) shows us how to be good wives (or husbands, if you're a man reading this book) and stewards in our marriage. You only have to listen for directions and instructions, and then obey what you are being asked to do.

Go on and fan into flame obedience to God and receive the man that He has for you. Whew!

"You're waiting for that magical day when someone makes the connection and recognizes who you really are. Maybe they'll first catch the sparkle in your eye. Or perhaps they'll marvel at your insights and the depth of your spirit. Someone who will help you connect the dots, believe in yourself, and make sense of it all. Someone who will understand you, approve of you, and unhesitatingly give you a leg up so that life can pluck your ready, ripened self from the branch of magnificence. Well, I'm here to tell you, your wait is over. That someone, is you." -Mike Dooley

THE WAIT IS OVER!

Teresa A. Stith

THY WILL BE DONE ON EARTH EVEN AS IT IS IN HEAVEN. AMEN.

Living God's Way...Purposefully

Lord knows, you will make mistakes! This time...go quickly to the Lord to fix it. The difference this time around is that we are not doing this thing on our own, we are including God in it. You have to practice turning things over to Him, because He knows what works best to have an effective and lasting relationship/marriage. Yield, yield, and then yield some more! Everything should become about God. This does not mean that you sit around like a zombie waiting for the Holy Spirit to zap you along. It simply means having an awareness that He is there! *Act* like He's there! If you're cooking dinner, ask Him which ingredients will best serve your taste and the one you're trying to please. If you're washing clothes, say "Lord, what kind of detergent can I use that will make the clothes fresh and soft?" The idea here is getting the Lord involved in whatever it is that we are doing. Whatever gifts you have, use them to make something nice for your husband. Sing him a song, plan a special event, etc. Ask God to show you what to do to surprise him, or to change things up a bit. Remember, God knows this man better than you do. When you include the Lord in every aspect of your life, you become accustomed to seeking Him and He becomes the forefront of every decision that you make. You begin to hear His voice more clearly and you EXPECT Him to speak to you.

You did not go through a period of singleness because God was punishing you for something. You went through this stage in your life because God was preparing you for something. There may be or have been areas in your life that God needed to heal. He needed to position you so that you could hear and obey Him. It was never to harm you, but to free you! God needed to get the attention of your inner man and awaken the Spirit in you so that you could be Spiritually led by the Holy Ghost and no longer controlled by your fleshly feelings and thoughts. You needed to be broken in some places and knitted back together by God Himself! What we have not understood is that God was doing for us during our singleness what we could not do for ourselves in a committed relationship. In your singleness, God needed to shift your focus from what you thought you wanted and needed for your life, to what His ultimate plans were for your life. As soon as you were able to accept His plans for your life, He was able to pull you into divine fellowship and show you a new way. Now, for the first time in a long time, you are able to hear Him clearly. Since He has your attention, pay attention to what He says, pay attention to how you hear, and be careful to follow all the way through with the instructions that He gives. It's not so that you can get any glory out of this, but that God can. This was all your period of singleness was for, that He could get the glory out of your life. That you put Him back in His rightful place, honor Him, acknowledge Him, and allow Him to live in and through you, to do of His good pleasure, is all God really wants. Sometimes this process can take years because God has to get to the root of your pain, your scars, your brokenness, your inability to trust, your fears, your guilt, shame, and all those other negative emotions that attached themselves to you. He has to rebuild your confidence and give you the courage to face yourself before He can send a man into your life. You cannot be any help to any man if you're broken.

One thing that helped me to live life on purpose was discovering the gifts that God had given me. Once I discovered what my gifts were, I began to invest time in sharpening my skills so that I could get better at them. I would have never thought in a million years that I would become an Author, but God used my talents to help me to stop giving so much time and thought to my past and my pain. Channeling all of my energy into my writing, gave me a break from wanting a man and helped me to focus on getting to know myself and what I wanted for my own life. In the process, I actually discovered that I looked good in colors other than black. I learned so much about myself. I discovered that I actually "liked" who I was and dug down deep to learn more about myself. God was slowly giving me my freedom back, something that the enemy had stolen from me years ago, and that I used "men" to keep me in bondage, thinking that I needed them to somehow validate me. The Bible tells us in John 8:36 that who the Son sets free is free indeed. I would have never discovered this freedom in Christ, if God did not allow me to become busy enough to stop looking at what I thought I was missing and work to create my own future in Him. I quickly learned what I was not looking for in a man. As I began to spend more time learning about the Holy Ghosts' role in my life, God began to pour so much of Himself into me and taught me what I should expect from a man who genuinely desires to be like the Lord. The man that we desire, and the one who God allows to chase after you should have the character of

God within. He should have the Lord's thoughts, and His ways. So you see, God knows what He is doing. Go through your process and be happy about it.   Prayer: Lord, let us live life on purpose seeking only to do your will. Help us to realize that when we choose to walk in obedience to you, Your blessings overtake us. Give us a mind to seek you in all of our ways. Help us to use our talents, gifts, and ideas to advance your Kingdom. Thank you for allowing us the space that we needed to grow closer to you in our singleness, and thank you for healing us from the inside out. Thank you Father for building our confidence in you and helping us to see ourselves through your eyes. Thank you that even when we could not see your hand at work in our lives, you were molding us and shaping us into who you created us to be at birth. Let us give back to you what you have so

Teresa A. Stith

freely given to us, a LIFE filled with all the Spiritual blessings of the Lord in Heavenly places, in Christ Jesus. Amen.

In ALL of your ways acknowledge Him, and He will make your paths straight

Proverbs 3:6

Financially Free?

There's plenty to do while you are waiting for your husband. What does those finances look like? I know, I know…we all expect God to send us a man who is already financially stable, but what are we bringing to the table? Don't waste your singleness! Rather than rushing God to send you a man, why not take the time to make sure that when he comes, he sees that you've been making just as much preparation for a life together as he has. Of course the man that God sends will take care of you and the house as the head, but we have to be willing to meet him half-way. I'm not saying that you should be rich, but I am saying that you should prepare yourself to be financially able to contribute to a life with the man that you love. Start now to ask God to teach you how to have a good financial foundation. The Bible urges us to "honour the Lord with our substance, and with the first-fruits of all of our increase (Proverbs 3:9). It takes wisdom to be able to save money and God freely gives it to us if we ask for it (James 1:5).

    I used to struggle so much in my finances that I wanted God to hurry up and send my husband, silly me. I used to tell God about all of the things that I wanted my husband to come with, that I never considered what my husband would be asking God for in a wife. I was so selfish with my requests. I didn't want him to have any kids, yet I have four that are grown. I did not want to deal with the baby mama drama.

Love Psalms to God

I prayed that he would only have eyes for me. As I think back to those requests, I realize that I was asking God to send this man with minus everything that the other men in my life had, so I was still somehow reliving the hurt that those guys caused me and even praying to God from that place. Once the Holy Ghost revealed this to me, my focus became more on healing rather than finding relief with another man. Our prayers should be in this season, that God will use our singleness to heal us where we are still hurting, and where we may still be broken. We may have been using a host of other things to cover up the truth behind our pain, but God wants to uncover the scars and heal them once and for all. Pay attention to your prayers. Sometimes we pray from a place of pain rather than a place of total freedom in Christ.

We may be in a financial bind due to unhealthy spending habits that stemmed from spending money on wants instead of needs. Ask God for wisdom to know the difference. I used to have a refrigerator full of food, but constantly chose to go out to eat just because I had the money. I basically wasted money being too lazy to cook. Now, I am not saying that there is anything at all wrong with wanting to go out to eat sometimes or to treat yourself, that is your right…but timing is everything. If you are short on cash, cook…period. This is why it is extremely urgent that we pray to God for wisdom. Wisdom teaches us how to live successful lives by using our ideas, knowing the Word of God, and operating in faith in what the

Word says. When we face financial difficulties or Decisions, it's the wisdom of God that enables us to overcome these challenges. There's nothing wrong with seeking financial advice from others. Make sure that it is someone that you feel comfortable sharing this information with. Building good relationships with others is necessary as we sometimes depend on others for our success. If we learn how to invest our time and effort into others, they will in return invest into us.

    Lastly, learn to give something away. God loves a cheerful giver! (2 Corinthians 9:7). A cheerful giver is someone who loves to give. Giving does not hurt, grieve, or put a strain on, but brings joy and happiness to yourself and others. This is one of the primary reasons why

God blesses us, so that we can be a blessing to others. When we pay our tithes and give a portion of our finances toward the work of the Kingdom, God makes provisions for us.

SINGLE LADY, YOU'VE GOT THIS!

What the BIBLE Says About Love

"Let the morning bring me word

of your unfailing love,

for I have put my trust in you.

Show me the way I should go, for to

you I entrust my life."

(Psalm 143:8)

Love does not insist on having its own

way; it is not irritable or resentful; it does

not rejoice in wrongdoing, but rejoices in

the truth. It bears all things, believes all

things, hopes all things, endures all things.

Love never ends

(1 Cor. 13:4-8)

Teresa A. Stith

Love one another
and be kind.

Love is never meant to be harsh or hard. Things will happen when God wants you with someone.

    Jesus was very clear on His stance when it came to LOVE and how we should love one another. As a matter of fact, the first and the greatest commandment is that we should "Love the Lord Our God with all our heart, and with all our soul, and with all our mind." And the second being just like it, "Love your neighbor as yourself." (Matthew 22: 37-39). Love worketh no ill to his neighbour; therefore "LOVE" He says, *is* the fulfilling of the law (Romans 13:10). You can only give as much love that has been given to you and as you allow the love of the Holy Ghost to permeate your heart, God's love will radiate and shine through you and abroad to so many others. Any attempt at loving others will fail without the love of God in you.

"A new command I give you: Love one another. As I have loved you, so you must love one another."

(John 13:34)

Your husband will love you easily when he recognizes that you are who God has chosen for him. He will be so grateful to God for you that he will want to die for you. He will love you and protect you at all cost and you will not have to worry about him looking in another woman's direction. He will give himself fully to you and it will not seem real at first, but this is how magical a moment this will be for you. You too will finally understand how God truly loves you, to bless you with a part of Himself to love you, honor you, and cherish you for the rest of your life. This is clearly "Love" on God's level and not what we (in our own minds) have perceived love to be. God's love is so high that you cannot go above it. It is so low, that it reaches way down to pull you up, and it is so wide that nothing or no one can go around it. What a joy and a praise that will envelope you when you discover it!

GOD'S LOVE FOR YOU IS PERSONAL!

And your husband's love will be the same way. No one will be able to interrupt the love that God binds between you two. His love will be a cherished love, a devoted love…a personal love…a love like no other. It will be no secret how intimate a love that you two will share. It will be so intense and so ignited, that those who dare to witness it will be caught in the heat of it, for it will be no denying that love does exist between you. THIS is LOVE on God's level. This love is REAL!

REAL LOVE
REAL LOVE
REAL LOVE

Teresa A. Stith

JUST BECAUSE YOU'RE SINGLE DON'T MEAN IT'S TIME TO MINGLE...

YOU HAVE WORK TO DO!

Your Single Self

Now that you understand what to do while you wait on the promises of God for your husband, go on with your single self and enjoy your single time alone with God. Let Him work His plans for your life into your life. Rather than complaining, now you can "thank Him" because at least you know what He's up to. FIX YOURSELF single girl and prepare your mind for what's about to take place. You've asked for it, now get ready to walk into it! Are you ready? Check and double check your attitude, your motives, your heart, and make sure that your husband can build on the foundation that you have laid for him as well as he for you. How can two walk together unless they be agreed? (Amos 3:3). Who wants to walk anywhere together and be miserable? This is not what God intended for love to be like. Get your house (your heart) in order! Consider that your man has prayed to God and just like you, have waited for this moment. He comes into this "love thang" with the expectation that you both have been waiting for each other, and this is the moment that you cease to wait and begin to express yourselves through your own acts of love and take the next steps in sealing your union together. What a MIGHTY God we serve!

    Go on and sing your LOVE PSALM to God and remember that when you first opened your mouth to tell God your desires, He heard you and went to work on your behalf. All that He showed you and told you were to condition you for what YOU asked for! So stop dragging your feet to clean up that house and wash those dishes. Stop spending carelessly and getting mad with God when He blows on your finances. Stop entertaining the foolishness of other men when you should be making preparation for your own. There's a blessing in every lesson and if your feelings are getting hurt while God is preparing you, then He still has work to do. Move yourself out of God's way so that He can give you what YOU asked for. Amen.

LOVE PSALMS

Teresa A. Stith

THERE'S A LESSON IN EVERY BLESSING... MOVE OUT OF GOD'S WAY

About The Author

Teresa is an "Author of Faith" who is always looking unto Jesus for that next book title.

Her books have brought motivation and inspiration to many lives young and old and she declares that she won't stop writing until God tells her to. God has given her testimony after testimony and she shares as the Lord releases her to. Her stories which were birthed out of her own struggles and trials have given others the victory in their own personal battles. Her new favorite scripture says "Wake up and strengthen the things that remain, which were about to die; for I have not found your deeds completed in the sight of My God. (Revelation 3:2)

More Information

Find this title and others at:

https://amazon.com/author/teresastith

Follow me on:

Instagram @afaiththatworks

Twitter @Afaiththatworks

LinkedIn @
https://www.linkedin.com/in/teresastith44b97512

Facebook

  @GodsReadyWriter1

  @Afaiththatworks

  @Faithittomakeit2

Join my group on Facebook:

bit.ly/thefaithgroup

BOOK REVIEWS HELP!

PLEASE LEAVE YOUR REVIEW ON AMAZON!

New and Upcoming Titles

Teresa A. Stith

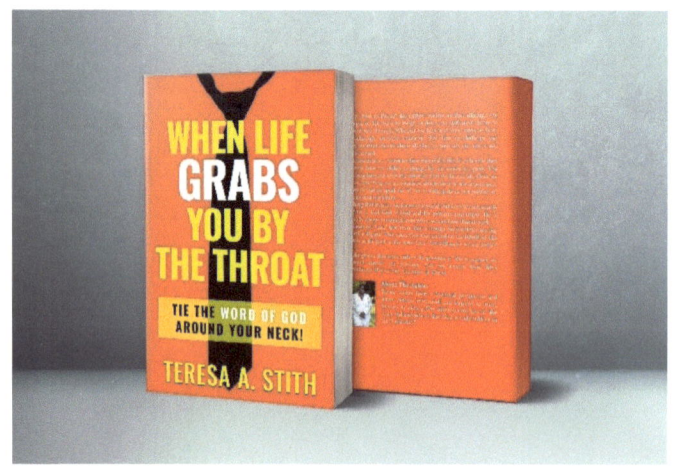

Love Psalms to God

FAITH WORKS WHEN WE WORK OUR FAITH!

Visit my website at

afaiththatworks.com

and my online store at:

faith-it-to-make-it.company.site

Teresa A. Stith

www.ingramcontent.com/pod-product-compliance
Lightning Source LLC
Chambersburg PA
CBHW042327150426
43193CB00001B/8